DESIRE AND WISDOM TO BE FINANCIALLY RICH

By

IMMACULATE MEDICI

ISBN
Hardcover: 978-1-964289-46-5
Paperback: 978-1-964289-45-8

INTRODUCTION

This book can help anyone to achieve wealth. It enables you to understand what you need in life to protect yourself and your family while moving in the right direction to financial wealth.

This book will help you with everything from the cost of retirement, accounting for inflation, building a solid portfolio of assets, and more.

While financial literacy and control are difficult to attain, it is not impossible, so there is no need to despair; if you read this book, you will always be a step ahead and in control of your finances and life.

Only you have the power to make this happen. Never allow anyone to make decisions for you. Take control of your destiny.

Table of Contents

Page Left Blank Intentionally

Chapter 1:
Analyze Your Wealth

I have read many books on how to get rich. I have found that sitting down and analyzing your life is the start of becoming rich. You can read every book on the planet, and it still will not get you to the goals of wealth you want to achieve. Sit down and analyze your financial statement. This will give you a clear understanding of where you are. To go forward, you must understand that wealth is measured in time, not money. You should have your money working for you, not spending all of your time working for money. It is very important that you set goals for where you want to be a year from now. If it helps, consider contracting some local universities to see if they offer programs on finances. Then and only then can you take stock of your finances and set your goals for wealth.

Let's get to the primary reason why most people have money problems. During your school years, you were never taught cash flow management. This is an essential aspect of life and should be taught to every child before so they are not sent into the real world blind and unprepared. For now, though, you will have to learn about it yourself. In doing that, you will learn that you do not need to work harder and harder for your money but have your money work for you. It is very important to know that more money won't solve your problems if you have a cash flow management problem.

You can find your score if you take a quiz on managing your money. Answer the questions below, and for every 'yes,' add 1 to your score. When paying your bills, are you always late?

1. If married, do you hide your bills from your spouse?
2. Does your family say you have a problem with overspending?
3. Bought something recently, knowing you did not need it and could not afford it?
4. Are you spending more than your paycheck?
5. Were you turned down for credit?
6. Do you gamble in hopes of getting out from under?
7. Have you not put off saving money for a rainy day?
8. Does your total debt exceed your income?
9. Are you overextended with your credit cards?

Now, add up your score. If you have a 0 score, you are well on your way to financial wealth. If you score 1-5 range you need to reduce your debt. If your score is 6-10, you are headed towards a financial disaster. If your score is high, it is urgent to increase your financial literacy and take control of your cash flow.

First, you need to establish short-term and long-term goals. This will help you map out a debt-reduction plan. As it is said, your first step is to pay yourself first. Take a percentage of any or all payments you receive. The operative word is "PERCENTAGE." Assign envelopes on saving, charity, and investing. Choose an amount you can afford to save, and at the end of the month, deposit the envelope with savings in a secure savings account in your local bank as an emergency fund. Do not take it out until you're ready to invest it in property, a car, etc. You will only be able to set aside money for these if you are good at controlling spending. Eliminate debt. Review your credit score. If you have applied all these steps, you can live within your means and are well on your way to financial security. That being said, you can move on to the next step.

The next step is to take control of your spending. Don't dig a hole so deep you cannot escape it. Do not be tempted to purchase things you do not need. This requires willpower. Rule of thumb: do not impulse shop. When you are about to buy something, ask yourself, do I need this, or am I getting it because I feel unhappy today? Shopping will make you feel happy for a short time. You will wear the item once, and then it will lay in your closet forever if you need a little help to trim your budget. Here are some ideas that can help you.

- Pay your bills on time and avoid late fees.
- Use one credit card until you're in control of your spending, and most importantly, set a limit for the expenditure.
- Find a credit card with a low interest rate, no annual fees, and no transfer Fees. Then, consolidate your debts to pay less interest fees.
- Pay off your credit card balances each month to avoid finance charges.
- Do not use ATMs that charge a fee. It's not a smart thing to Pay for your own money.

Try to shop smart. The intelligent thing is to pay cash whenever you can. Use Your card only for emergencies. The old saying is, "If it's not broken, don’t fix it.” That goes for your home appliances, car, etc. Don't go to the stores to buy on impulse. Wait for sales.

- Shop at discount department stores.
- Vacation only if you have Money.

- Cut back on eating out.

Take control of your spending. It's very important, or you will not recover from debt. How to dig yourself out depends on your liabilities. If you have unsecured debt, you must get free of it. Examples of unsecured debt are personal loans, medical bills, and the charges on your credit cards. If you do not have a credit card, do not borrow from a friend or family member because your debt becomes their asset and your liability.

Getting free from your unsecured debt will take time and patience. The interest charges are compounded daily. The sooner you start a reduction plan, the better. You must have a strategy.

If you have saved money for a rainy day. Then, use that money to pay your debt. If you can find a credit card with deferred interest for a year, try to transfer the amount to the credit card with deferred interest and pay it off as soon as possible. When you have paid off your debt, close that account and keep only one major credit card for emergencies. And when you use the card, continue to pay it off each month. Consider seeing counseling. Because this may be a chronic problem, you need help from an objective outsider who is open to your problem. They may tell you to change your relationship with money and how you think about it. If you consider not getting help, your achievement will be short-lived.

The bottom line is that you must take responsibility for your actions when spending money. And don't try to live like the Joneses. Know the difference between good debt and bad debt. Get rid of the bad debt and increase the good debt, and you will be on your way to financial freedom.

Let's sum up this chapter with this mantra.

I chose to be rich.

I will educate myself on how to make sound financial decisions.

I will take advice if I find myself getting stuck and find myself falling off the wagon.

I will take control of my finances and empower myself to think differently about money.

Change the way you think about your life and finances. Change your attitude and find out which one help you and which one will hold you back.

If you need help, don't be afraid to ask for it. Remember, we are only human, man, and mistakes are made by the best of us. No one can do it alone.

You will find that everyone needs help at one time or another. Changing your thinking will help you, and asking for help will get you down the right path to financial wealth. Be grateful for everything you have. You are in this universe for a reason, not alone. Consider your choices in life and that you will make the right ones. And you will have no problem going down the right path to financial wealth.

Chapter 2:
Portrait of a Millionaire

The factors of getting wealthy are the person who owns a small factory, a chain of stores, or a service company. You will find that he or she is married once and remains married.

They live well below their means and live next door to people with a fraction of their wealth. Together, husband and wife are compulsive savers and investors.

They dress to impress but wear inexpensive suits and wait for sales. They drive American cars. The wives are planners and budgeters. Remember, charity begins at home. They accumulate enough wealth to live without working for ten years or more.

They are fastidious investors. They invest nearly 20 percent of their household income each year. You should hold two percent of the household's wealth in transaction securities and mutual funds. Put as much as you can in a pension plan or 401K.

You should understand that if your goal is to become financially secure, you will likely attain it. But if your motive to make money is to spend money on the good life, you will never become wealthy.

Building wealth is not something that changes one's lifestyle. It should only be the security in one's mind that one can keep a certain lifestyle and have no worries.

P.A.W. are builders of wealth- that means they are best at building net worth. Typically have four times the wealth accumulated. What is P.A.W., you ask? Well, there are three types of wealth accumulators, and they are:

- P.A.W. (prodigious accumulator of wealth).
- U.A.W. (under accumulator of wealth).
- A.AW (average accumulator of wealth).

Be goal-oriented. Keep daily, weekly, monthly, annual, and lifetime goals clearly defined.

You will find that having goals will make you financially independent. And a financially independent person is much happier than someone who is not financially secure.

You should not overspend. To build wealth, you must minimize your realized (taxable) income and maximize your unrealized income (wealth/ capital appreciation without a cash flow). Invest heavily in tax-free municipals, sheltered real estate, and stocks with unrealized gains to minimize tax You can say that practicing being a tightwad to a certain degree can minimize your wealth.

Chapter 3:
Be a Tightwad

"Tightwad" means being someone who has money working for them. It is keeping the lifestyle you want to be accustomed to, not struggling, and not living from paycheck to paycheck.

Let's target some people's problem: spending too much and going out of control. It may help if you can put together a daily list. Every time you spend in the course of a day, write down each item you purchased. Look over your list and analyze each item you have spent on. Ask yourself, with each item, did I need this item, and what does it do for me? Most of the time, you don't need it, and it doesn't make you feel any better than you felt before you purchased the item. So, you haven't accomplished anything by buying it, but you have put yourself in debt. Repeating this action over and over again will only put you into deep debt to the point of bankruptcy. It's like they say- never go grocery shopping when you are hungry. The same goes for other shopping. Never go shopping when you feel sad, depressed, or vulnerable because you will go out of control in shopping, and if you think about it after you have shopped, you do not feel any better, and I assure you, you are worse off. Think about the shopping when the bills come, and you will realize you have sunk to a new low and have a more severe problem. All this causes you more problems.

Your credit score will be affected, and you don't want that. Someday, you may want to buy a house, but you won't be able to because there will be repercussions every time you try to get a loan. A downward spiral will be imminent if you can not take control of your actions before they take control of you. The bottom line is to think, analyze, and make the right decision. So, seek professional help. And you will be better for it. Don't stress it because if you seek help, you are admitting and addressing the issue, and that's the first step to fixing it. That is a sign that you are headed in the right direction to wealth. Just take it day by day because it never goes away that feeling of out-of-control shopping. You only need to take control; don't let it control you. Imagine living in the upper rich class. When you retire, all you need is to set a goal. While you are working, put away as much money into your 401K. That will be a start or a guideline for you to work with. Make up your mind and set goals. I have found that whenever I want to accomplish something, whether to buy a home or a car, I want it so bad that I can taste it. I give myself a certain amount of time and ensure I can accomplish that goal in my set period. Planning and controlling are critical factors in wealth accumulation. You must operate on a fairly well-thought-out annual budget. You must be frugal.

Investing at least one-third of your yearly pre-tax household income is very important. That being said, you must live below your means. Being frugal is the cornerstone of wealth building.

You cannot build wealth if you have a lavish lifestyle.

A great offense is good for the young men, but you need a defense. The cornerstone of accumulating wealth is a great defense, and you should follow with budgeting and planning. This is a little harder for guys because, as a man, you always pay when you take a girl out on a date. But you are headed in the right direction if you plan and budget.

If you have a problem planning and budgeting, don't be ashamed to ask for help from a professional budgeter or planner.

I was told that knowing about finances is the direct and simplest rule to wealth.

I would ask you to do a simple test. Multiply your age with your annual household income (not including inheritance). Divide by ten. This less your inherited wealth is what your net worth should be.

For example: Your annual income is $55,000.00

Your age is 56 years old.

$3,080,000.00 divided by ten is $308,000

My net worth should be $308,000.00 when I am at 66 years of age. This is just an example. And with the cost of living going up, it changes every year. But you should get an idea of what I am trying to say. To achieve financial security and tranquility, you must change your way of thinking about money. You must say to yourself no more living paycheck to paycheck. Be firm in your decision, move forward, and don't look back. Take control of your finances. Do not let your finances take control of you.

You can only acquire budgeting and self-control skills if you work at them.

Just a reminder. The example I have shown you above is just that, an example of what you should save for your golden years. But remember, as we live longer, we should save more. The cost of living goes up every year. Allow that in your equation. Think positive and let no one tell you differently. You and you alone can achieve financial wealth. Never second-guess yourself. You will find that a little hard work will bring its rewards. Be thankful every day for what you have been allowed to accomplish.

The day I chose to be rich, I remembered sitting down and analyzing my life. I knew where I was, but I had to decide where I wanted to be five years later. I gave myself five years because it gave me time to plan. I worked building up my credit and paid off all my debt. Then, I proceeded slowly, purchased a vacant lot in Florida through a corporation, and made monthly payments until I paid it off and received the deed. I bought the lot for $12,000.00. I kept it for a few years and then decided to sell it to move on to my next project.

Oh, by the way, I sold it for $50,000.00. Not a bad deal. I then went on to purchase a two-family house with a commercial store. I got a loan and was well on my way to becoming wealthy. I held the property for over ten years. Of course, I collected rent, worked with my tenants, and kept the property up to par. I kept the property in excellent condition because I aimed to sell it within ten years and get a reasonable price. I did sell the property and went on to purchase another. This time, it was a five-family with a store. You see where I am going with this. For me, it was property. For you, it can be something else. Whatever you can dream can and will be true if you want it bad enough. You must prepare yourself for opportunities that come your way. And if possible, go for it. Of course, you must have self-control. Don't go into a project with your eyes closed or with the attitude that making money is another way to spend uncontrollably. Because if that is your objective, you will fail and lose everything. Be responsible in your decisions. Remember, when it comes to financial matters, it's essential to keep your eyes and ears open; you must realize where you are, and you will spot the opportunities when they cross your path. Remember to do your homework, collect all the information required to purchase property, and open a business if you wish to work for yourself. Then, you are on the right track to becoming rich or financially secure.

As you get older, your income should increase. Do not depend on a pension and social security because it will not support you in your retirement age. Social security might not even exist in the future with how our government is going. Becoming rich or finding a financial security cure is never too late. It's up to you. When you are ready to make the change amazing things can happen if you want it bad enough. Remember, if an idea is in your head and you keep thinking about it, then you can turn that idea into cash. You and only you can make the changes in your life for the better.

Think positively, do your homework, plan, talk to a

professional if necessary, and then go for it. Only if you feel comfortable can you make the changes in your life for the better.

Life is about making mistakes and learning from them. I have made mistakes, but the secret is not to repeat the same error. You must learn from that mistake and correct it to work in your favor. Don't let anyone criticize you, put you down, and talk you out of making the move. You and only you can decide what is suitable for you going forward and making something of your life. Remember, life is what you make it. Think big, and you will succeed in your financial riches.

If you speak to a rich person, they will tell you they did not get where they are today on their first try. Yes, they ran into many disappointments and failures. They did not accept failure. They looked back and learned. They then prepared to mentally react calmly to their failure and moved forward. Yes, you guessed it- they tried again. Yes, you fall, but you pick yourself up and try again and again until you get it right. And despite all your fears, follow your heart, and you will succeed in anything you want and set your mind to. As soon as you change your thinking from negative to positive, be confident, and commit to whatever you wish to do, it will happen, and you will be on your way to becoming rich because you chose to become rich. It won't hurt to read financial magazines, go on the internet, and get informed from financial literature to understand better how to build your riches. Everyone needs some type of help now and then. The bottom line is that taking control of your finances will empower you to a new life for yourself and your family. Open your eyes and ears to the information out there, and it will create a new and rich life for you and your family. Choose to be rich, and you will have financial freedom.

- To sum up what we have learned:
- Think positive, and you will embark on the road to riches. Have the courage to act despite the fear.
- Be creative to think outside the box.
- Have the self-confidence to withstand criticism.
- Have self-control and be modest, keeping a level bead.
- You can't accomplish anything if you set your mind, heart, and soul to it.
- Most importantly, be grateful and give thanks for being allowed to accomplish what you set out to become.

Remember, we have a choice to do right or wrong,

and you are the only one who can make that decision. It won't hurt to take the time to be thankful.

When looking into the mirror, you must stand tall and tell yourself three important quotes.

I come from greatness.

I attract greatness

I am greatness.

Chapter 4:
Think Positive

Looking in the mirror reflects your inner thoughts and what you believe in your soul. Listen to your thoughts and think positively to go down the road to riches.

Don't make excuses for yourself. It's much more difficult to make excuses on how you can't become rich than actually to achieve wealth. Stand firm and educate yourself so you won't stumble over your financial matters and fail. Keep an open mind and take in anything and everything when someone is trying to educate you for success. Everyone needs some help at one time or another. There will be some disappointments, but don't let it stop you. Just get up and try again and again until you get it right. If you find your passion in life, that is half the battle. It will make you feel confident and enthusiastic in accomplishing your quest. You should continue working at your job while putting together your life's passion.

Be persistent in absorbing all the lessons you can acquire. When you feel confident to open your own business go for it. If you think you should start, then start part-time, and it won't hurt to stay at your job for a while until you feel confident. Remember, Rome wasn't built in a day. Having a baby takes nine months. You get what I am saying. You must first build a strong foundation. If you don't, it will tumble down around you. If you want to become rich and hold on to it, you need a strong foundation and financial literacy knowledge. Take some courses in college on finances. It wouldn't hurt. Take the leadership in your life to learn and go forward on the road to riches. While you are learning, you will come across individuals who are mentors, coaches, and advisors who can teach you valuable skills needed to own your own business. You can build a team for your business and work together to succeed.

Remember a very important saying:

"WHATEVER THE MIND CAN CONCEIVE, IT CAN ACHIEVE."

Think big, put it out to the universe, and it will happen. To attract money, you must focus on wealth. You must think in abundance, and you will tip the scale in your favor.

Think positive, feel good about your thoughts, and think big.

Things will happen for you. And there is nothing you cannot do or accomplish.

You are the master, the boss of your destiny. Believe

you have received it; the law of attraction is so powerful that it will move heaven and earth to get it to you. I have demonstrated that theory, and it worked for me. I often spoke to the universe about owning and repurchasing my first property. Whenever I asked the universe what I wanted, it came to me. If you do your homework, you will find evidence that anyone who accomplished anything in life did not know how they would accomplish the task. They only knew that they were going to do it no matter what. They have come in the form of a mortgage broker, an attorney, and a real-estate agent crossing their path, and they will make things happen. Think of yourself as a magnet attracting everything you want, and it will come to you. Have trust, believe, and have faith in yourself. You only need to ask, and it will happen.

They say that if GOD brings you to it, he will bring you through it. That is my belief. You were born for a purpose; begin to expect great things to happen to you, and it will shape your life before it happens. Make it a habit to shape events in your life in advance through your thoughts. And you will see that you are creating your life exactly how you want it to. Your life is the result of your thoughts. If you think negative things won't go well. If you think positively, you will find that things will go your way very smoothly.

When you desire something, make it known to the universe, and it will come into your life. I have found that everything I have accomplished in my life, I owe it to the man upstairs. Every morning, I thank GOD for giving me the chance to accomplish what I have accomplished and allowing me to accomplish more going forward.

I am grateful for everything I have. Being grateful will only bring me more accomplishments in my life. You have to visualize having what you want, and it will come to you. On a wall, put a whiteboard; cut out pictures of what you would want in your life. It will be all the goals you wish to accomplish. Put that board in a place where you will always see it. You will find that your thoughts will come true and acquire what you want. As you receive it, be grateful for acquiring it. Remove old pictures and put new images on the board when you wish for a new goal. I have done this, and my goals have come through. Expectation is a powerful thing. If you want, you will acquire. Be grateful for acquiring it, and thank the great all mighty for helping you. Being thankful sends a powerful signal out to the universe.

I know and feel that what I have said is very powerful, but it is true for everyone who desires to achieve goodness in the world. That goes for accomplishing wealth.

It has been said. Give, and you shall receive. The

wealthiest people give to organizations. Be generous and responsible in giving, you will find that the universe will open up, and riches will pour out. Philosophy, gratitude, caring, being thankful, positive thinking, and love are all connected with you and the universe. It's essential that you understand that, and you will attract the riches of the world. You need a strategy for how to create money. Find what interests you and do what it takes to accomplish your goal. I had found that real estate was my passion, and I took the steps to find the property and apply for a mortgage. I was on my way to becoming a landlord. A family member was passionate about opening a business repairing office equipment, and in his first year, he made his first million. And back in the 70's, a million was money. I also worked for someone who sold cans of soda on the beach when he was a young boy. But his passion was to own commercial buildings in New York City. His father was a maintenance man for one building, but one day, he told his father he would own the building his father worked in. Sure enough, he did and owned many more buildings in New York City. I know an attorney who has a passion for helping people. Today, he has a lucrative business. Find and work with knowledgeable people, and you will reach your financial goal. Have the passion, and you will be on your way to riches and financial freedom. Be grateful, thankful, and modest in your journey; you will find that the universe will magnify you with all the riches you desire.

Think big, never stop dreaming, and believe in yourself. Never let anyone put you down or have second thoughts if you do the right thing. People who make you second guess yourself are jealous of you and don't want you to achieve your goal. As they say, misery loves company. Don't let misery in. All the examples I have given you are authentic. It can also be true for you if you open up your thoughts and allow the universe to show you how to accomplish your goal and set you on your way to riches. Work with people who have accomplished their passion and are wealthy. Because they have set the path in the right direction and can show you the way to financial freedom. Trust your instincts and allow yourself to incorporate your ideas, also. As you learn, you will open up new roads to riches and financial independence. The most important thing is to accomplish your wealth of financial liberty for you and your family. The tranquility would be very rewarding. You should allow your children to see and understand how hard you have worked for their interests so they will be grateful for everything they have gotten. That is the secret of the universe: be grateful and say thank you for everything you've acquired, and it will attract more great things to you.

As I had said at the beginning. All the millionaires you have come across are people who desire to be rich. They take it one step further. They acquire knowledge themselves with the necessary tools to succeed in life. You must desire to make money, for those who did not go to college do not despair. You, too, can become rich if you desire it. Don't get me wrong. College is critical, but some of us are not college material, and that does not mean we cannot become wealthy. It's the drive, the desire, and the willingness to want to become rich that will get you there.

Real life is a different kind of learning experience. In your life, if an opportunity knocks, grab it before it slips away. Do your homework. Find out what type of business opportunity is in front of you. Ask yourself: Do I know anyone with an idea or a business you can help expand? Remember that you will make decisions that cost you lots of money and decisions that will make you lots of money. Learn from them to minimize your losses on the next adventure you wish to tackle. Adopt a pattern in life and focus on wealth. Balance your standard of living and work at producing the desire and the capability to acquire wealth. Life is a balance of experiences: you can choose to be wealthy or poor. It's up to you to make that choice. Have a strategy to get the knowledge that is needed. Write down the pros and cons of investing your ideas, the cost, and what it would take to start. You are on your way to plan your destiny. The most important thing is to plan your future, become successful, and not limit yourself.

Chapter 5:
Your Purpose

Aim high in your expectation. Believe in yourself that nothing and no one can stop you. Give yourself a time limit and ensure you are ready when that time comes. If it helps, read some books on successful people. You will discover that most of them lost and tried repeatedly to accomplish the right path to wealth. Trying repeatedly until they got it right only made them more appreciative. The most important reason to create wealth and to build a business is for you and your family's wellbeing. You need something that will pay you much longer after you stop working and are in your golden years.

Remember, the government does not care about you and your family. Social Security that you have paid into may not be there when you retire. Our government is corrupt, and they will not be there for you when you are in need. This is why you must take action in directing your life on the right path to wealth for you and your family. If you want to reach the status and enjoy the freedom that comes with it, you must take steps to accomplish financial freedom for yourself and your family. And remember to be grateful and thank GOD for your accomplishments.

Let's be honest we need to take responsibility for our life and our family's life. Remember, there will be no one you can count on except yourself. Think positive and stay focused to secure a comfortable life for you and your family. Your life will have more meaning and tranquility if you have financial security. The greatest gift you can give yourself and your family is financial security. When you focus your thoughts on what you want and hold that thought, you are summoning what you wish to with the universe. Thinking positively, the universe will give you what you are asking for. You can create your life through your thoughts. So, you must think positively because you have no idea how powerful you are. It's important to know that GOD has a purpose for you and a mission in life. So, it is essential to go down the right path to secure your life and finances for you and your family. You have the power within. You can attract all the good and riches you desire with your wisdom. There are many roads to go down, but you and only you can pick the right road be because GOD has laid the path for you. You have the free will to do good things for yourself and create your destiny. You were put on this earth for one reason: to do great things. It is up to you to seek happiness, wisdom, love, and compassion within you to radiate it to others, and it will come back to you in many ways. Whatever obstacles got in your way in the past only prepared you and made you stronger to continue bringing you to the present to do good for you and your family. You have the power within you to be whatever you wish to be. But you must think positively because you have no idea how powerful your thoughts are. And if you embrace it and share it with others, you will be blessed many times. Do whatever you love. And if you don't know what that is, just ask the universe, and it will present itself in many forms or ideas. Remember that when you ask for guidance, it is equally important to give thanks. Every day, give thanks for your health and wealth. Remember, GOD'S NOT DEAD. He is genuinely alive and there for you, no matter what happens. He will help you in your quest in life. He will guide you down the right path and be on your side until you complete your journey.

Remember, there is a purpose in life for you. It's to make the world a better place for you and everyone who crosses your path.

It's essential to understand that every one of us has a purpose to make our world a better place to live. Think of the good you can do; letting others follow you will be magnificent for the universe, and the universe will give back to you in many ways. Give yourself a chance to experience the abundance the universe will provide you with. The joy and the wondrous you could experience that the universe has for you. Good health, good wealth, and the pleasure to experience it all. Be aware of things around you, stop smelling the roses, and enjoy what you do daily. Give yourself a break, and don't take things too seriously. Know that many will be there for you if you let them. In searching for wealth, let people who cross your path help you achieve your goal. Reward yourself and others who help you achieve your goal. No man is an island, and everyone needs someone to guide them in the right direction. Everyone who has achieved wealth has gotten help at one time or another.

Look back on all the famous people you have read about and what they accomplished in their lifetime. They had powerful thoughts, and they released them into the universe. The magical thing is that the universe attaches to those thoughts and sends them back to the source, and things start to happen. We are connected with the universe. Think big, and it will happen for you. Don't give up because if you don't succeed, try and try again. Remember, the law of attraction is the law of nature. If you think positively, then positive things will happen to you. If you feel negative, negative things will happen to you. It's that simple.

The first step is to ask, the second is to believe, and

the third is to receive. I have always believed that whatever I had asked for, I have received. It may not happen quickly, but make no mistake, it will happen. That is why you must be positive in your thoughts because of the law of nature; whatever you ask for will be granted sooner or later.

Remember the old saying, "Don't want something too badly because you will get it." There is no time limit on when it will happen because when and only when you are aligned with the universe, the law of nature, will it be allowed to happen. Use your ability to think positively, be happy, be grateful, have love, believe in yourself, and beautiful things will happen to you. If you accept great things in life, you will create and direct your life to be great. Learn to create every event in your life through your thoughts, ahead of everything you do and everywhere you go. If you think that way, you will intentionally create your life in a great direction.

Remember, there is you, a magnet, and the universe. Whatever you project into the universe will manifest and come back to you in many ways. The only thing that is asked of you is to thank and be grateful for what you have received. Keep in mind the universe asks very little of us in return, but it grants you tremendous rewards.

You are here for one purpose: to do good for the

earth, the universe, and yourself. Be thankful for everything you do and every day for being able to do it. I have read of people finding themselves living a good life, and one day, their lives are shattered. Whether it be money or maybe a spouse leaving, a mother finding herself as a single parent or a loved one passing, they found themselves not knowing what would happen. They sat down, analyzed the situation, and started to put their lives in perspective by thinking big and asking the universe for help, believing it will happen and receiving and, most importantly, thanking before time so when it happens, they will be ready to receive it.

There have been great teachings on thinking positively and throwing out the universe so that someone's life can improve. If you do not believe me, read some books- go to the library there are many subjects on this matter. These people have started companies selling creative things that make your life easier and, in return, have made their lives easier and profitable. They choose to give, and their returns have a multitude. They no longer have to worry about their future and the future of their children.

Every night, when you go to bed, list the events that were not so great and make changes to create more extensive and significant events planned for the next day. Before you sleep, make sure you are grateful for everything that has happened that day. And every morning, say, "Thank you".

A little gratitude must go a long way.

Chapter 6:
Real Estate

Let's talk about real estate. We need to view the long-term of our housing market. First, you need to ask yourself what you can afford and how much of a down payment you can put down. There are points you should consider to lower the interest rate. Should you put down a smaller down payment? If so, consider paying a higher interest rate and insurance for the mortgage. Also, your credit score determines if you are eligible or not. It would be smart to check your credit score. There are major credit bureaus: Equifax, Experian, and Trans Union. Getting information from all three is important because not all creditors report your information. It's also very important to get a credit score, which is a computer-calculated number. The higher the number, the better your chances of getting a mortgage for a home when you are ready to buy. Typically, a score of 660 or higher qualifies for a conventional or "prime" loan; below that, the borrower is considered a higher risk.

Prequalifying for a mortgage helps determine how much you can afford. A real estate agent will run your numbers through a prequalification calculator to determine which home to show you. You will also have to consider closing costs. You must decide if you can pay them at the closing or finance them by taking a slightly larger loan or accepting a higher interest rate. Do your homework, don't accept your first offer. Get a few offers and go with the best one. Make sure the state banking department licenses the mortgage broker or lender and that they have no complaints on their record. Also, getting a lawyer to represent you is very important so everything can go smoothly and there are no surprises. Many horror stories have come out after the home buyer closed on the deal, and they could not do anything about it. One big example is a lien on the home from property taxes, water bill outstanding, etc. Only a lawyer can find out these hidden horrors. The money you spend will be well worth it in the long run. And your lawyer will advise you not to sign anything you do not understand.

Going forward, I will detail how having a lawyer you trust will mean that most of the work is done for you. That will be the only true and secure way to own your own home, and it will be an AMERICAN DREAM. For some people, they find themselves wanting to own their own home because it creates a sense of security. Renting is not enough security for some. They are at the landlord's mercy, not knowing how high the rent can go if and when they can get evicted if the landlord sells the house. It also gives them the secure feeling that, if nothing else, they have a tangible asset where they can sleep at night. This is part of your financial riches for your golden years. A home appreciates in value and it can be a lifesaver for you and your family going forward. If you need to sell your home in your golden years, you will get great profit on your investment. A bank will never give you the return that a home will.

As I've mentioned, it's challenging to keep track of all the different mortgages available in the market due to varying rates and terms. Here is a list of some different mortgage options:

1. Adjustable-rate mortgage: This offers slightly below-market interest rates, which is beneficial for beginners. However, payments can increase significantly when the index rises.

2. Balloon mortgage: Payments are based on a fixed interest rate, usually short-term, and may cover interest only. This is suitable if the homeowner anticipates selling or refinancing within a few years.

While there are more mortgage types, the best one is a fixed interest rate if you plan on keeping the home for the long term. With equal monthly payments of principal and interest until the debt is paid, it provides stability and long-term tax advantages. The only downside is that the interest rate may be higher than other types of mortgages. It's crucial to choose the best option for you, ask questions, and seek advice from professionals.

Emphasizing the importance of doing your homework, it's advisable to engage with a good lawyer. They will initiate essential paperwork, accompany you from the sale to the closing, ensure all documents are signed and recorded, and conduct a title search to verify the seller's legal ownership without any liens on the property. Though the process is laborious, the satisfaction of realizing the American dream is unparalleled, making it the best investment you can make with great returns in the long term.

To recap, follow these steps:

1. Choose an area to live in.
2. Allow time to save a 10% or 20% down payment.
3. Select a good lawyer to guide you through the entire process.
4. Get preapproved to understand your affordable house range.
5. Find a reliable realtor agent willing to show homes within your price range.

Achieving home ownership provides security and

peace of mind for you and your family, contributing to financial security. The rewards are substantial, and it's essential to express gratitude. Don't hesitate to ask questions, do your homework, and make decisions only when you feel secure and confident in understanding the responsibilities of owning a home. The sense of accomplishment and security that comes with being a homeowner is unmatched, giving you a reason to be thankful every day.

Staying on track and managing your finances wisely is crucial. Consider yourself a small business enterprise with both inflows and outflows. Money comes in and is spent on necessities like food, shelter, clothing, and various other items. Budgeting is essential. Begin by totaling your income and then itemizing your spending. At the end of this exercise, determine whether your spending surpasses your income. This should be a part of your daily routine, especially considering the uncertainties in our economy and the apparent self-interest of our government.

Learn to save and let your money grow through interest. Consult with an expert at your local bank who can provide information on effective money-saving strategies. Budgeting daily is a practical way to save money. Consider bringing lunch from home and giving up costly habits, such as a pack-a-day smoking habit, which can accumulate to

$3650.00 per year at $10.00 per pack. Similarly, avoiding buying coffee out can save $1820.00 per year at $5.00 per cup.

These examples demonstrate how adopting millionaire-like spending habits can help you avoid living paycheck to paycheck. Teach your children the importance of wise spending and responsible money handling. Encourage them to take on part-time jobs to develop financial responsibility. When obtaining a credit card, choose wisely and use it only in emergencies. Opt for a credit card with rewards, such as cashback on restaurants, grocery stores, and gasoline bills. Be mindful not to let credit card usage spiral out of control. Pay your bills on time to save on interest payments.

By following these ideals, you can lead a financially stress-free life and work towards an enriched and happy future for you and your family. This approach puts you on the right track for retirement. Adjusting your lifestyle can make things more carefree, and common sense is key to making the right choices. Educate yourself, and you'll be on the path to financial security. As always, don't forget to give "THANKS."

Chapter 7:
Start a Chain Reaction

Banks hold your money for your safety, a practice that has been in place since your parents' and grandparents' days when the government had a genuine and honest agenda for the American people. In those times, the American people were prioritized, and banks adhered to rules, with bank staff knowing their customers on a long-term basis and looking out for their interests. I remember accompanying my mother to the bank in the 1950s to 1990s, where the agents suggested the best accounts for their clients, fostering trust and enabling them to make profitable long-term decisions while safeguarding customers' money.

However, after the tragedy of September 11, a decline in respect, integrity, and honesty for the American people was observed, and those born in America felt they had lost their voice. Witnessing this decline, I chose to invest in real estate. My first purchase was a piece of land in Florida through a big corporation. Purchased it for security for my future. Then, I purchased a second piece of land in Florida with the notion of building a home on it. But decided not to build; instead, I purchased a condo in Miami and sold the piece of land for a down payment on my condo. This is just a little insight for you to ponder. It becomes a chain reaction. Starting with small investments, establishing credit, and obtaining a mortgage for a dream home became possible with patience, imagination, courage, self-control, and self-belief.

It's crucial to be smart, diligent and educated before making any life decisions. Establishing good debt by purchasing a home that appreciates in value provides equity for future needs. Borrowing from this equity should be strategic, such as for buying another home, not for frivolous expenses like a car that depreciates in value. Investing in your home, which appreciates over time, is a path to long-term financial security.

In your golden years, if you've managed your home equity wisely, you can sell your home for a smaller property or condo, banking the rest for your preferred lifestyle. Money in the bank alone may not make you rich, but investing in your home can lead to financial prosperity, allowing you to live in your golden years with self-respect.

Taking responsibility for your financial security and creating a legacy for your loved ones is a wonderful accomplishment that deserves gratitude. Being gracious, humble, and thankful for your achievements can go a long way. You are interconnected with the universe, and by expressing gratitude and asking for what you desire, you align yourself to receive the help you need. This process may take time and manifest in various ways, but with determination, you can achieve your goals.

Your purpose on this earth is to do good and accomplish significant things for yourself and your family. Teaching your children to follow suit creates a chain reaction that continues through generations, contributing to the betterment of the world.

To parents, teach your children the responsibility to save for their future. Encourage programs in their schools to have a saving club for each child during the school year so each and every child can save and monitor their money. This will help them find a feeling of pride and importance in their lives. I mention this idea because when I was in elementary school, we had this program for each and every child; it gave us a feeling of financial freedom and importance. I helped at home with my chores and was paid. I would take a percentage of the money and put it in a savings account. At the end of the school year, I was given my passbook. Going to the bank, my mother and I found my money plus interest accumulated. I could then do whatever I wished with the money.

Going to school, you are taught academic courses but no teaching of financial security for everyday life. Get involved in your child's school with interests that public education does not cover. I feel that if this is addressed to the children, they will be willing and ready to embrace it. It will give them an incentive to want to go to school each and every day. We find that a child does not easily listen to their parents. They feel that parents preach, and it's not cool. But if you implement this program in their school, each and every child will embrace this program with open arms. It teaches them common sense.

When I was young, times were different, and our interests in life were different; our parents worked hard to teach us the importance of survival in everyday life. Things were much simpler then. One parent went to work, and one parent was home to make sure our needs were filled. There was a secure interest at all times in a child's life. Today, both parents have to go to work, and life is hectic and fast-paced. So, a child does not always have the luxury of having good advice in everyday life.

It is a good idea, and you're going in a positive direction to financial wealth for your child, and it will have a secure impact on his or her life. In the long term, they will be very thankful you have taught them to help themselves in real life. Be proactive in your child's life. Too many people are living paycheck to paycheck these days. It is sad because you get a feeling you are in a sinking ship. It's not a good feeling, and it does not motivate anyone to get up in the morning to go to work.

At work, you are entered into a 401(k), which allows you to have money taken from your paycheck and put into a savings account. And to make it more interesting, your employer will match your money, sometimes dollar for dollar. That is a good practice and makes you want to put some of your pay into that program.

It is also exciting to know that it will not be taxed until you are allowed to withdraw it at age 59 1/2. These rules are done for your good. It allows you not to touch your money until you retire. Remember, all this is good for one's ego. It makes you feel that going forward, your life will be much more tranquil. You have to agree life does not get better, but it does get harder. Our government leaders are very greedy and mistrustful. They are only concerned about themselves; the bottom line is how rich they will get. They promise to be concerned about the taxpayers, but in reality, they are only concerned about themselves. We have to fend for ourselves and make smart moves for our future and for the future of our children.

Remember the saying, and I quote, "GOD HELPS THOSE WHO HELP THEMSELVES." Be grateful and give thanks each and every day. Each and every time you give thanks, you open a path to the universe to arrow back to you your wishes and desires. Take life into your own hands and make the right decisions for you and your family. It will give you great pleasure to pursue the good things in life and achieve great financial wealth in your life for you and your family. Keep a positive attitude in your life. You may fail once, twice, and maybe three times, but it will make you stronger when you finally do achieve the financial wealth you have worked so hard to accomplish. It will keep you grounded and help you make sound decisions going forward in your life when you do find yourself financially wealthy.

Never stop trying and help others accomplish their dreams. Remember what was given to help you achieve your financial wealth must be shared with others who want to achieve theirs. When you get, you must give, and that is full circle, as they say. I truly believe that if I am helped, I feel compelled to help others. When you get, you must give. It's not so hard to understand. You can call it a chain reaction.

Chapter 8:

Give and You will Receive

The universal truth that has stood the test of time is, "The more you give, the more you will receive." This principle is ingrained in us from childhood and is considered a law of nature. To attract more tranquility, wealth, and happiness into your life, dedicate more of your time and attention to helping others, and you will find that others will reciprocate.

Another well-known saying is, "Treat others as you would like to be treated." Despite living in the greatest country, the United States, there's a sad reality that millions of people still do not know when or where their next meal will come from, lack proper shelter, and face the heartbreaking issue of homelessness. For the most prosperous nation, this should not be our legacy. Despite being considered leaders of the world, we often spend money on lavish things we do not need, purchasing to impress others. It's disheartening that buying things for the sake of impressing others speaks volumes about us and can lower our self-esteem.

Before you can help others, you must help yourself

and your loved ones. Charity starts at home. There is a need for responsibility. Choose what you need in life, not just what you want. Once you've helped yourself and established responsibility, you can then give your time and money to help others to help others feel happiness and confidence. This follows the rule of the universe: the more you give, the more you will receive.

Let's be more responsible with our lives and the lives of our loved ones, as no one else will look out for them. This is not a dress rehearsal; you go through life only once. Make it great, enjoy the journey, and fulfill your values. Making life fun for yourself and your family requires honesty, both with yourself and others. Believing in yourself is crucial to connecting with others and establishing bonds for a rich financial life.

I myself started enjoying my life late in life, having the idea that enjoyment would come after retirement. However, in the present generation, the mindset has shifted. You can enjoy your life from the beginning, ensuring that you haven't missed anything by retirement. Start today by asking yourself, when did you last experience joy in your life? Be honest with yourself to make a change for the better.

Ask yourself what makes you happy at work, home with friends and family. Find what you love to do. Do not be afraid of failure. Because those failures will teach you and direct you on the right path to success and financial riches. Find what works in your life and what does not. Ensure and strengthen the right things and eliminate the wrong things in your life.

And put it in writing so you can go back as a reminder to stay on the right path. You have been put on this earth for a reason. Everyone has a purpose here on earth. It's up to you to find out what your purpose in life is. Be true to yourself. Do not judge yourself or others too hard. Make sure to pursue fun in everything you do in your life. It's not easy to live life carefree and with no problems. But if you are honest with yourself, you can tackle each problem head-on and with ease. Teach your children the correct way to live by your mistakes. Help them be more responsible with finances.

Help them save more and spend less. Teach them not to make it important to impress others. Teach them to love themselves and find value in life for themselves and not for others. Teach them to be thankful for everything in their lives. Take nothing for granted. The first thing in the morning and the last thing in the evening is to thank GOD for what they were able to achieve in life. They must be true to themselves. And they must be true to the universe. Then and only then good things will start to happen in their lives.

Enjoy your journey. Do not take things too seriously in life. Respect life, and it will respect you. The financial riches are within your grasp. You need only to ask and it will be granted.

There are so many ways to get rich. The one way I found is taking advantage of buying real estate. I started late in my life, but I did find riches. I knew that working 9-5 was not going to make me rich. So, I decided to test the waters into real estate, and the money flowed my way. I started to buy condos near the beaches. My first condo was at the Jersey Shore. I rented it seasonally, made money to keep the property going, and banking some money for a rainy day. I then purchased a condo from a friend in Myrtle Beach. I rented it, collected rent to keep the property going, and banked the rest for a rainy day. I purchased a condo in Orlando, Florida, near Disney. I also rented it to keep the property going, banked some money for a rainy day, and repaired the condo. I also enjoyed these condos for myself. I had a place to go when I was on vacation. My Orlando condo had three bedrooms and two baths. It was a beautiful unit. I then sold it and doubled my money. I then invested the money in another property in another part of Florida (Miami South Beach). I invested in a condo in Vegas, which is rented on a daily basis, and a check comes in the mail every month.

For the Vegas condo, I purchased in a new development that attracts people from around the world. I also branched out to Maryland and purchased a one-bedroom condo fully furnished, and I have it rented year-round or what is called a long-term rental. A check comes every month; I use part of the money to pay my bills on the condo and bank the rest for a rainy day.

After 9/11, the local government promoted real estate development in difficult areas to get tax abatements to encourage developers to build in less attractive areas. And, of course, it was passed down to whoever purchased the building. In some unattractive areas, purchasers felt so happy to have their property taxes reduced by as much as 90% over 10 or 20 years. They actually saved a total of hundreds of thousands of dollars. If you are thinking of owning your own business, it would be wise to own the building to house that business. That is the only way you will get rich. Many franchises practice this rule when considering opening their business. Most of the time, your mortgage payments will be less than what you would pay in rent. In some cases, you can look into what the government can offer and what programs they have to help you invest in real estate. All this is possible if you have the interest and the patience to work hard to accomplish your goals in going forward on the road to getting rich. You need to work hard and be diligent. These are some of the ideas that will make you rich. Working hard and living a meaningful life will make it easier for you and your family to live a happy and tranquil life in retirement.

Chapter 9:
Live Smart

Remember, living smart will make life happier for all. You will be able to sit back and tap into your retirement funds without being penalized. Let's go down the road to riches.

To spend wisely, save more, and invest while still young. The best strategy is to save long enough for big purchases like a car or house so that your payments and other expenses won't exceed 50% of the net monthly income. Each and every time you get an increase in your pay, try to direct the money to a savings account or an investment account like a 401K.

Most importantly, try to distinguish the differences between wanting and needing something. Cut back on spending on monthly expenses. Check cable bills, internet, phone, and eating out. I bring lunch daily to work; you should try to do so because you'll be surprised how much money you can save each week.

A typical lunch can cost you $10.00 to $15.00 per day. One week's breakfast can cost you $50.00 X (multiplied) that 52 weeks can cost you for one year,

$2600.00. One week's lunch can cost you $75.00 X that with 52 weeks, and you'll find the cost of lunch is $3900.00 per year. All in all, it can cost you per week for breakfast and lunch $125.00, and for one year, it can cost you a sum of $6,500.00. You'll be shocked at how much money you can save in a year's time.

Put that money in a savings account or invest in your 401K to generate positive cash flow. Always set your sights on saving when you are young because it will come in handy when you are in your golden years. Remember, life gets harder when you get older, and having a comfortable pillow to fall on will mean a lot. It could mean having a roof over your head instead of being homeless because you could not meet your rent or have enough food for yourself and your loved ones. I know it is harsh to think that way, but if that motivates you to save, then it's not so bad to think that way. Remember, the government will not be there for you when you really need them. And you cannot depend on your children because they have a life and a family to care for. It can't hurt to be responsible when you are young. You will be smart in thinking that way for your own sake. And as I said in the past, be thankful. Give thanks for what you have accomplished in your life every day.

I have always focused on accumulating assets like

OWNING LAND. Purchasing land in a great location, I bought land in Florida (Port St. Lucie). The same location where the Mets practice each year. I purchased it just before they came. The price I had purchased the lot for was $12,000.00 dollars.

OWNING LAND

I kept the lot for a few years with the intention of building a home on the land. The lot had a wonderful canal in the backyard. My reason for purchasing was to invest and, when I was ready, build a home on the land or sell it for a profit and purchase a home in another location in Florida. So, I decided to sell the lot and sold it for a whopping profit of $50,000.00 dollars. I then invested it as a down payment for my first condo.

OWNING CONDOS

I then started to invest in purchasing condos. My first condo purchase was in Virginia Beach, a wonderful two-bedroom condo. I hooked up with a realtor and had them rent the condo for me. I then collected rent each month, waited for the economy to improve, and put the condo up for sale. And yes, you guessed it, I made a profit. I sold it for $95,000.00 dollars. I then invested the money and purchased another condo on the Jersey Shore. Do you see where I am going with this? It becomes a chain reaction. There is always money to be made when you are determined.

OWNING MY OWN HOUSE

I was blessed to own my own home. I have a two-family home, and to help pay my bills, I rent one apartment and live in another. The feeling of security is fantastic, to say the least. Everyone can own their own home.

OWNING A BUSINESS

If you have a strategy in your life, go for it. Thinking of opening a business? Go for it. Small businesses are the backbone of this country. If you are good at something, put it out there and make money. It can spiral into other good things in your life.

Remember, all of the above generate positive cash flow. Some feel owning a car is an asset, but the reality is that it's not. It does not generate positive cash flow, and you will find that as soon as it's driven off the car dealer's property, it decreases in value. It doesn't mean you shouldn't own a car but know the difference between positive cash flow and negative cash flow. Educate yourself, and you will be on the right path to financial wealth. And again, be grateful and thankful for your achievements.

Chapter 10:
The Benefits of Saving

Practice better money habits. Sit and collect an inventory of your credit cards and how much you owe. Add how much you earn per week, meaning how much you bring in. If you are spending more than you earn, you must correct that. Look at the average amount of money you earn over a lifetime. Take the time to figure out how many years you are or will be working. Multiply that by your yearly income, and you will be amazed at how much you will be worth in your lifetime. How you manage your money can make a difference in becoming a millionaire or not. Ask a financial planner about the easy changes you can make to move further along the road to prosperity.

I understand we are talking about a weekly paycheck. After taxes are taken out and the bills are paid, there seems to be nothing left to save for your retirement. But what is left, you can take another portion of that money and put it in your savings towards financial goals. Then pay your bills. What is left is yours to do whatever you wish. Remember that when I say save, I am not suggesting a large amount. Take small amounts each week, be consistent, and you will find the path to financial wealth. The amounts can be $25.00 to $75.00 per week. Each time you get an increase in your paycheck, increase your savings accordingly. The important key is to live below your means.

At your job, make it a habit to put as much as you can in your 401K because your employer matches your amount. There is also a new program with a health program that your employer can set you up with so that you have a health savings plan before taxes. The money you save in the health savings plan can be carried over from year to year, and you will have the money there for doctor's visits. Doing this will put you in a different tax bracket. It will allow you to pay less taxes and keep more of your money or keep more for yourself and less for the tax collector.

I would suggest making this a family project. Teach your children to save on a regular basis because as long as you are there for them, they will be fine. But someday, you will not be able to help them, and that is when they will be in trouble. And remember, you are in control of your money and your future. Never allow anyone to tell you differently. Stay on top of your goals, and make sure you follow through. When you reach retirement age, it will be harder to save, and that is when you need the money to survive because our leaders in government will not be there for you, no matter how good of a taxpayer you are. It's very important to encourage your children to follow in your footsteps. That's the best gift you can give them. Allow them to be creative and come to you with suggestions, and if you feel it's not good for them, then discuss the pros and cons with them. Let them feel encouraged to come to you and not be afraid to speak to you about their ideas. Remember, they learn from you, and you learn from them.

And as always, give thanks for what you have.

I have tried to express different ideas on how to save. That being said, it all comes down to managing our finances and educating ourselves. Stop using credit cards; try using cash. As my dad used to say, if you do not have the cash, don't buy the item until you have saved enough cash to purchase it. He lived by that rule all his life. My mother used to cut out coupons when she needed to go to the grocery store. Try not to eat out all the time.

If you must open a credit card, open one that rewards you, whether for fuel, travel, or your groceries. Open a bank account and save a percentage of your pay for a rainy day. Also, open a Christmas club, collect a gift, and you will find that you saved enough throughout the year to purchase gifts for your children at Christmas. If you need a cell phone, get one with no contract plan. Your local Wal-Mart has good plans that may help you save money.

During my childhood years, we did not have the luxury of a dryer. Yes, we had a washer, but we hung the clothes outside on a clothesline. That alone will save you on your home's high gas and electric bills. Having a yard, we grew our own tomatoes, peppers, onions, and greens, saving us some money. Watching my pennies has helped me save. There's an old saying: "Watch your pennies, and the dollars will take care of themselves."

If you must use your credit card to buy food, make sure you can pay the balance in its entirety when the bill comes to avoid paying high interest. Credit cards offer one or two percent cash back; applying it to your balance when you pay your bill can help.

I cannot stress this enough: if you live below your means, spend less, and save more, you will be fine and are on the direct path to financial security. If you have a job and they offer you a 401K, and if your employer matches what you put into the fund, go for it because it's a good deal. Start as early as possible. The earlier you start, the less you need to save each year. You will have a longer time to accumulate. Each time you change jobs, you can roll over your 401K to your new job. You can speak to a certified financial planner to better understand these plans. I wish I had started earlier, but my job in my younger years did not offer a savings plan. You see, I worked for family; they did not offer plans like big corporations do. I started at age 40 and tried to save as much as possible, and then the stock market tanked. I saved as much as I could. I did okay but could have done better.

Like I said, get a company that matches your contributions; it will help you become a millionaire much faster. Pay attention to your employer's investing schedule. Read the fine print because you need to be fully invested. To keep your employees' contributions, you may have to be employed with the company for, say, five to six years. But that's not so hard to do.

I do not encourage you to bounce from job to job. There is one drawback with a 401K; you cannot withdraw money from the account until you are 59 1/2. There is an early withdrawal fee if you do. But that is a good thing because when you're young, you can work and make a living, but that money is for your golden years when you can no longer work. Remember, the government will not help you when you are in need. Educate yourself, and ask questions about what is the best portfolio you can put together. As your fund becomes larger, try to diversify by mixing stocks, bonds, and cash that are right for you at your age. Life can be beautiful if you find the best road to your financial goal.

Allow yourself to communicate with the universe; you will find the answers you need. Be thankful each day; you will find that life can be easier.

Let's sum up what we have learned so far. As you know, for most people, holding down a job and earning a paycheck is pretty much their way of achieving financial security. But just working won't do. The secret to attaining financial security is to turn your income into wealth. You need to convert your earnings from your job into savings and invest in long-term investments. You should start saving a percentage of your earnings; it can be 10% of your paycheck regularly. As your pay increases, your percentage should increase along with it. If you follow the regiment over the long haul, you can end up with a six to seven-figure nest egg by retirement. Then, you can sit back and enjoy your golden years.

One obvious way is a 401K from your employer. You should set it up where it is automatically taken out of your paycheck before taxes. Not only would you be in a lower tax bracket, but it would also get you started on your financial goal. Suppose your company does not offer a savings plan. In that case, you can invest in a program that can transfer funds into an IRA account or a taxable investment account with another investment company. I opened an American Trade account, purchased stocks, and put money into a money market. I was able to save close to a six-figure nest egg. I invested in a 401K, and in my years working with the company, I managed to save close to a six-figure nest egg there, too. Don't worry if you are one to move from job to job; you can transfer your funds to your new company without penalties. As I explained in the early part of this book, you can calculate your income with your age close to retirement, get the sum, and divide it by ten years. It should give you the amount you need for retirement. How great is that?

Chapter 11:
Pathways to Financial Wealth

Let's face it, there are times when you want to give up, but it's important to stay the course. Gradually accumulating about three months' worth of living expenses in a savings account, in addition to your other savings, will help you avoid dipping into your long-term investments. The trick is to stay focused and committed to your long-term strategy. I promise you, it will be worth it in the long run. If you find it helpful, write down your long-term goals; it may make it easier to stay the course.

I've read that the rich have a secret to getting and staying rich: they set their sights on a goal, not on people or things. They maintain a positive attitude at all times. Thinking like a victim will never attract wealth. Your attitude toward money will reflect in your bank account. The saying "reap what you sow" really does ring true. Kindness begets kindness.

Knowledge is power. Read books on financial wealth and any other books on wealth available in the library. Indulge in reading all you can; you'll find that setting goals is a common thread among the wealthy. Keep your promises to yourself and never give up on your dreams. While we all face money challenges, it's true that overspending and living beyond our means can exacerbate our problems. Start small, set achievable goals, and work on them one at a time. Educate yourself on the money mistakes to avoid.

When you set a goal, see it through to the end. Start it, work on it, and accomplish the result, then move on to the next goal. By doing so, you'll achieve financial wealth in your life. Have fun along the way, and be thankful for your accomplishments. Remember, the wealthy focus on one goal at a time. They let no one get in their way, follow their gut feeling, and associate with positive people in their lives. Nothing is impossible for them. They may fail, but they get up and try again until they succeed. They refuse to let defeat bring them down; they keep fighting and trying until they get it right and achieve financial wealth.

We all understand that adopting a millionaire mindset is pivotal in the pursuit of wealth. Hard work and persistence are essential, but achieving financial abundance also demands diligent preparation. It's perfectly acceptable to seek guidance, ask questions, and educate yourself on the principles of success. Every wealthy individual has, at some point, undertaken the task of self-education and sought advice from the right sources. Rest assured, by committing to this journey, you're laying the foundation for financial prosperity.

Many have amassed wealth without the traditional route of attending college. While education is undeniably valuable, some individuals may lack the means or inclination for higher education. However, with unwavering persistence and dedication to your goals, financial wealth is attainable. Maintain a positive mindset, write down your goals, and keep them in plain sight to reinforce your commitment every day. Positive action and personal empowerment invariably yield positive outcomes. Remember, while money is a tool, true happiness stems from love, spiritual fulfillment, and contentment. Resist the temptation to let money dictate your life; instead, take control of your finances and cultivate gratitude for your achievements each day.

Embrace gratitude for life's blessings and cherish your relationships with loved ones. Approach your journey to financial wealth with the right mindset, finding joy in the pursuit of your goals. Though the quest may seem daunting, remember to infuse it with enjoyment and reward. When you invest effort into your endeavors, you'll develop a profound respect for money and its potential. Contrastingly, those who inherit wealth without effort often fail to appreciate its significance. Find fulfillment in the process of earning your wealth and revel in the satisfaction of your accomplishments.

Avoid procrastination and self-doubt, as hesitancy may cause opportunities to slip away. Understand that passive inaction will not lead to wealth; it requires diligent effort and unwavering commitment. Embrace the challenge, knowing that through hard work and dedication, financial abundance is within reach.

Chapter 12: Strategies for Long-term Success

There are numerous avenues to achieve financial wealth, as discussed earlier in this book. However, the most crucial step is gaining control over your spending habits. When you see a branded item in a commercial and feel the urge to possess it, pause and reflect. Ask yourself, "Do I truly need this, or am I simply influenced by peer pressure?" More often than not, it's the latter. It's imperative to track both your spending and income realistically, setting aside funds to initiate wealth-building endeavors.

Investing a small portion of your earnings won't suffice to build significant wealth. It requires disciplined investments in secure avenues guided by professionals. Working with a knowledgeable financial advisor can steer you toward stocks with compound interest and market growth potential, eventually leading to a comfortable nest egg.

Establishing an emergency fund is crucial for unexpected expenses, such as car repairs, home maintenance, or sudden unemployment. While the average recommendation is two to three months' worth of expenses in a short-term deposit account, a more prudent approach would be to save six months to a year's worth for added security.

Optimizing your portfolio for tax efficiency can save you thousands annually. Consult with your accountant before making any significant moves to avoid unforeseen expenses. If you're interested in global investments, seek guidance from a professional financial advisor. Investing strategies may vary based on age and risk tolerance, so adjust your approach accordingly.

Remember, the opinions expressed here are solely those of the author and not necessarily endorsed by financial professionals. Seek expert advice tailored to your specific circumstances before making investment decisions.

It's essential to express gratitude daily and recognize your role in the universe. Cultivate habits of gratitude, as they attract wealth and abundance. Learn from others' experiences, both successes, and failures, to carve your unique path to wealth. Train your mind to embrace wealth-building strategies and maintain focus on your goals.

Start small, test the waters, and continue to pursue wealth-building opportunities while maintaining stable employment. Avoid rushing into ventures without adequate preparation, as setbacks can be costly. Believe in yourself, work diligently, and express gratitude for your achievements. With perseverance and a resilient mindset, financial wealth is within your grasp.

Celebrate financial freedom and break free from the cycle of living paycheck to paycheck. Refuse to deny yourself the wealth and prosperity you deserve. Simply believe with enough conviction, and you can attain the abundance you've always imagined. Remember, our creator placed us on this earth with purpose, desiring us to achieve all the financial wealth we can envision. Dream without limits and banish fear from your life, for it is the greatest obstacle to the fortune that awaits us.

Begin by eliminating debt once and for all, and commit to living within your means. If you lack the funds to purchase something extravagant, pause and question whether you truly need it or if it's merely to impress others.

For me, expressing gratitude and seeking guidance from a higher power each day has been paramount. Through faith and prayer, I've found divine inspiration and the courage to pursue my dreams. While my beliefs may differ from yours, whatever drives and motivates you is valid.

I've remained diligent in seeking guidance from a higher power in every aspect of my life. Despite making mistakes and experiencing failures, I persisted, driven by a heart set on goodness. Diligence and hard work are rewarded by nature's law, ensuring that during tough times, new opportunities emerge. By asking for blessings, remaining grateful, and doing right by others, lasting financial wealth can be attained for oneself and one's family.

Helping others is a powerful act that brings both personal fulfillment and universal abundance. Have you noticed how doing good for someone else uplifts your own spirits? The universe reciprocates such acts with abundant blessings. Wealthy individuals often advise pursuing one's passions and expressing gratitude to the universe daily.

Chapter 13: Overcoming Regrets

Like many of you, I blame myself for not having started earlier in life. I know I began late due to laziness, irresponsibility, and the belief that marrying a wealthy man would solve my financial problems. But regardless of the reasons, I've made a pact with myself to only look forward and not dwell on the past. It's unfair how we beat ourselves up over what we haven't done or should have done, endlessly lamenting the mistakes we've made in our lives.

When I ventured into real estate, I often found myself dwelling on missed opportunities. How many times have I thought, "If only I had bought that house for $350,000, now it's worth $1,500,000"? Others second-guess themselves for passing up low-priced stocks that later skyrocketed. We need to stop being so hard on ourselves and refrain from the "coulda-woulda-shoulda" mentality.

Negative thinking only blinds us to present opportunities. Humans are fallible, and mistakes are inevitable. Instead of dwelling on our errors, we should learn from them and ensure we don't repeat them. Focusing on the past only perpetuates it into our future, dragging us down and obstructing our path.

To overcome regrets, we must confront them head-on, acknowledge our mistakes, and take responsibility for them. Only then can we release them to the universe and allow positive changes to occur in our lives. Our brains are incredibly adaptable and capable of being reprogrammed. Our thoughts shape our reality, so cultivating a positive mindset is crucial.

Make your journey enjoyable, and give yourself permission to be imperfect. Don't succumb to self-doubt or second-guessing. Trust your instincts and make decisions confidently, knowing that failure is merely a stepping stone to success. Many successful individuals have faced setbacks but persisted until they achieved financial wealth.

Each person has their method of releasing regrets. Some write them down and burn the paper symbolically. For me, it was about persevering until I achieved my goals in real estate, owning commercial properties, and enjoying the passive income from rents. This journey towards financial security and independence liberated me, fulfilling my purpose in life.

You're not meant to merely exist; you're destined for greatness. Don't fear failure or setbacks; they are part of the journey to success. As Americans, we're fortunate to have the freedom to pursue wealth and achieve our dreams.

Books on finance can offer insights, but true change comes from within. If you're reading this book or any other on financial wealth, it's a sign that you're ready to transform your life for the better. Trust in yourself, embrace change, and embark on the journey to financial freedom.

Chapter 14:
The American Dream

Living in this country (America) is a blessing. We're endowed with freedom—the freedom to pursue our dreams and be whoever we want to be. Each of us is unique and has a purpose on this earth, and it certainly wasn't to live in poverty and struggle. While money doesn't guarantee happiness, the lack of it can certainly lead to misery. As a baby boomer, I can attest that financial constraints make it challenging to enjoy life to the fullest. It's a reality that should concern everyone, especially when contemplating our golden years. We all desire a future where we can live without worrying about bills, putting food on the table, or enjoying well-deserved vacations.

That's why it's crucial to start thinking about finances early on and how they'll impact our later years. We don't achieve our desires through mere wishes; it takes action and determination. Our choices and actions shape our lives, regardless of when we start. Many have begun their journey to wealth later in life, investing their time and resources wisely. It's about thinking creatively and persevering through the inevitable ups and downs.

While it may seem easier to live paycheck to paycheck, it won't lead to the fulfillment of our dreams. For me, it instilled a drive to take action and invest in real estate. I started small and gradually expanded my ventures. We all aspire to a better life, but it's crucial to learn from those who've achieved financial success. Plan your journey wisely, taking the first step and acting upon it to attain the life you desire.

While pursuing your dreams, keep your day job and explore other opportunities. Maintaining stability while testing new waters is a prudent approach. And remember, setbacks are inevitable, but it's essential to pick yourself up and try again until you succeed. Trust in the universe and its ability to provide, but also understand that action is required on our part.

There are numerous paths to wealth. For some fortunate individuals, it's winning the lottery, but let's face it, that's not guaranteed. However, if you're willing to put in the effort, there's a surefire way: while working a full-time job with the benefits of a 401(k) and health plan, you can also establish a second income stream by becoming your own boss. Many people successfully juggle entrepreneurship with their day jobs, often in partnership with a spouse or family member. The next generation of millionaires is emerging by creating wealth from home, particularly leveraging internet expertise.

Regardless of your interests, there are various side business opportunities to explore. Men and women alike can offer services like small construction work or start home-based ventures such as baking or crafting jewelry. Freelancing is another option, whether in architecture, graphic design, or other fields. Those with a knack for antiques can refurbish and resell them, while real estate enthusiasts can pursue a second career as a part-time realtor or property investor.

Government-sponsored training programs can help you kickstart your entrepreneurial journey, and even family members can contribute—children can take on newspaper delivery jobs, for example. The possibilities for earning extra income are endless, from babysitting and grocery delivery to seasonal tasks like snow removal or lawn mowing. Even committing just a couple of hours per day to a side hustle can yield significant returns.

Starting your own business is encouraged by the government as it fuels economic growth. By thinking creatively and exploring unconventional avenues, you'll pave the way towards financial security and success. Trust me, thinking outside the box will lead to a brighter financial future.

There is a popular website called eBay, known for its auction platform, and it offers the simplest way to start a small business from home without quitting your day job. With millions of people visiting the site daily to buy various items, it's a surefire platform for selling goods and creating a home-based business. Here's how you can generate a second income while maintaining your day job:

I had a coworker who, while working her day job, would purchase designer clothing on sale and resell them on eBay, making a nice profit. Many people dabble in internet sales and find success, and you can do the same. As the saying goes, "One person's junk is another person's treasure," and eBay is utilized worldwide.

Another option is Amazon, where you can buy books and a wide range of items, similar to eBay, and also sell goods to generate a second income. If you love animals, you can start a dog-walking business. Simply introduce yourself to your neighbors, distribute business cards, and you're on your way to earning extra income.

If you're serious about starting a second job, you can turn any hobby or passion into a money-making endeavor. Be creative and think outside the box. Even if your initial attempts fail, don't give up. Analyze what went wrong, adjust your approach, and try again. Many wealthy individuals didn't succeed on their first try; persistence and determination are key. You have the power to achieve financial wealth—just put your abilities into action, follow through, and never give up until you reach your goal.

While it may seem daunting, remember that you're here for a reason, and failure or poverty is not your destiny. With freedom of choice, you can accomplish anything you desire in life. Dream big, aim high, and persist until you achieve your goals. Enjoy the journey, be grateful, and trust that the universe will guide you in the right direction.

Today, we have access to numerous incredible free websites on the internet. Among the approximately two dozen useful sites available 24/7, my favorite is "Get Free Stuff." This site offers a plethora of links providing everything from coupons to free movies and books.

In the financial section, you can discover websites that help you calculate your net worth. Simply fill out an online form provided, and you'll find out your worth. Other useful features include:

- Financial planning: Create a financial plan tailored to your needs and your family's.
- Finding banks: Find banks with the best interest rates for certain deposit amounts.

- Annuities: Learn about the best ones to buy and the questions you should ask about them.
- IRA: Protect your IRAs, 401(k), and other retirement accounts. Get information on what to do when you retire and how to safely roll over your 401(k) to avoid penalties.
- Social Security: Apply for benefits, request a Medicare replacement card, and more.
- AARP: Access the most informative magazine on health, wealth, and leisure time.

Discover amazing freebies and deals safely and easily. Additionally, find websites and state and federal agencies that help locate unclaimed assets. Many people abandon assets when they move or switch brokers without claiming their money. You can contact the abandoned-property office in your state and provide your correct name, social security number, maiden name, nickname, and previous addresses to inquire about any unclaimed funds. Be sure to contact each federal agency directly, including the IRS, Social Security Administration, and Bureau of Public Debt.

If you need to fix up your home, there are grants available. Contact the Rural Development office in your state to apply for a loan or grant. While there may be restrictions, don't let that deter you from trying. There's nothing to lose—just ask, be optimistic, believe in yourself, and things will happen.

Keep your day job, but have a strategy in life. It's important to start a retirement savings account, whether it be a 401(k), traditional IRA, or Roth IRA. Allocate a portion of your pay and save it for retirement. Educate yourself—there are numerous ways to achieve your goals without needing lots of money. Government grants are available. Find your passion in life and pursue it. If your passion is to solve world problems, create jobs, or make the world a better place with new inventions, you may be eligible for a grant.

The government assists people with grants who want to help themselves and society improve and lead better lives. If you have an idea that can benefit others, visit a government website, search for grants, and follow the instructions. There may be applications to fill out, but you have nothing to lose. Apply yourself, maintain a positive attitude, believe in yourself, and go for it. The only thing that matters is following your dream or passion. Let nothing stand in your way. Never give up until you achieve it.

Remember, even the most successful entrepreneurs have failed multiple times before succeeding. They persevered until they got it right. Real estate was one of my passions, and I tried repeatedly until I succeeded. I started by purchasing a condo, made a small profit selling it, and moved on to the next project. I achieved each goal while keeping my day job for the benefits. I chose real estate because it didn't require my presence 24/7. You may choose a brick-and-mortar business or start a website and run a lucrative business selling products or services.

Whatever interests you, go for it. Put your all into it at the beginning, ensure it runs smoothly, and then you can sit back, relax, and watch the money roll in. It's not all about the money, but it can make your life and your family's life much easier going forward. What matters is that you can take care of yourself and your family without depending on government assistance. Welfare is a handout, but achieving your goals and accomplishments through your own efforts is satisfying.

You know that you are here for a greater purpose and shouldn't lower yourself to depend on the government to dictate what you should or should not do. Think big, aim for the stars, stay positive, and never give up.

Chapter 15: Embracing Second Careers and Financial Independence

Baby boomer are part of the revolution. As a Baby Boomer myself, I've realized that the cost of living is soaring, leading me to focus on real estate investment for my retirement. I began dabbling in real estate while maintaining my day job, which provided medical benefits and sustained my daily expenses. Real estate became a supplement to my primary income, offering additional profits to secure my retirement. I transformed my passion for real estate into a profitable endeavor, learning and enjoying the process, ultimately securing enough funds for my golden years.

Finding your passion and turning it into a business is crucial. Many people spend their entire youth working for others, enriching their bosses, only to realize that investing in their dreams could lead to equal success. However, fear often hampers individuals from trusting their judgment and investing in themselves. Yet, many Baby Boomers are breaking free from this fear. After retiring from their 20 or 40-year day jobs, they have taken the time to reflect and analyze their current situations.

Transitioning from a life of constant work to having ample free time can be challenging. Many Baby Boomers, feeling unfulfilled during their golden years, have embarked on second careers after turning 60. They've returned to school, leveraging their life experience to pursue new opportunities. Some have found that what once brought them joy can now be a source of income. The key isn't necessarily making a fortune but finding enjoyment in what you do and supplementing your social security income.

It's widely acknowledged that a monthly social security check isn't sufficient for comfortable living. While politicians in Washington retire in luxury, funded by taxpayers' money, ordinary citizens are expected to make ends meet on meager budgets. This disparity is exacerbated by taxation on already limited incomes. However, Baby Boomers are urged not to succumb to governmental constraints. Instead, they should invest in themselves, empowering their own decision-making and seeking new opportunities.

Reinventing oneself and seeking family support in this journey can lead to personal and financial growth. Remember, each individual has a purpose, and the universe encourages progress, perseverance, and prosperity.

Our time on Earth is temporary, and during our journey, we're tasked with making the best decisions possible. It's believed that God desires our success and prosperity, urging us to help one another along the way. Giving and aiding others is not just a religious doctrine but also a fundamental law of nature.

To attract more wealth, tranquility, and happiness in life, the key is to give more. This doesn't necessarily mean donating money; rather, it involves giving more of ourselves. Everyone possesses expertise in something, and sharing that knowledge can create a chain reaction of support and assistance. The super-rich often share this common trait—they are givers. This principle, akin to the golden rule of life, suggests that the more we give of our time and resources to help others, the more we receive in return.

In my own life and the lives of those around me, this principle has proven true time and again. Even a small gesture can make a significant difference. For instance, donating a portion of profits from a business to a reputable charity or volunteering time at a local shelter can have a profound impact.

Giving of one's time can be particularly gratifying and meaningful. Whether it's assisting at an animal shelter, serving meals to the homeless, or helping a neighbor with errands, these acts of kindness foster a sense of self-gratitude and enlightenment.

Respecting and caring for one another sets us on the path to financial wealth and personal fulfillment. By following the "golden rule of the universe" and giving freely, we discover our true worth in life. Simply ask the universe, and it will provide what you need to thrive.

Chapter 16: Trading Wisdom – Insights from a Decades-Long Journey

If you're serious about finding a way to make money, consider investing in profitable software that can teach you how to use the computer effectively. Overcoming your fears is crucial for success. Set clear goals for the future and maintain discipline in your life. Learn to control spending risks and manage your money wisely. Develop a positive strategy and stick to it without second-guessing yourself. Align yourself with the universe rather than resisting it, and enjoy the journey with a positive attitude.

Maintaining steadfastness will significantly impact your outcomes. Strive for nothing less than the best in life and maintain a healthy attitude. Psychology teaches us that a positive mindset combined with persistence leads to success. Wealthy individuals embody this attitude, allowing nothing to hinder their progress. Embrace losses as learning opportunities and continue trying until you succeed.

Give yourself enough time to achieve your goals and express gratitude along the way. Remember, the universe supports those who strive for success, whether you believe it or not. Successful and wealthy individuals don't just work for money; they leverage their resources to work for them. Study how wealthy people achieved their success, and you'll discover it requires hard work, a positive mindset, self-belief, and unwavering determination.

Always keep an open mind and be willing to seek help when needed while offering assistance to others. Collaboration is essential for success. Remember, the fundamental principle of the universe is that when you ask, you will receive. Similarly, when you give, you will receive. Never underestimate the power of the universe. Work in harmony with it, and you'll find that things naturally fall into place.

Let's discuss the stock market. Over the past 10 to 20 years, I've dabbled in trading. I began with Charles Schwab and later switched to TD Ameritrade, setting up accounts with both. Starting small and proceeding cautiously, I immersed myself in books on trading. However, I learned that even the best resources couldn't accurately predict market movements.

Successful trading demands discipline and the ability to discern when to buy and sell. I aimed to purchase stocks at their lows, monitor them, and sell at their highs. Initially, trading was enjoyable, but the crash around 1999 changed that, leading to substantial losses. Despite setbacks, I persisted, adopting a long-term approach. Over time, my account rebounded and even exceeded previous losses.

The key to trading success is maintaining composure, enduring market fluctuations, and adhering to the adage of buying low and selling high. It's a challenging endeavor, as the market is beyond our control. Attempting to fight it often results in losses. Instead, align with market trends and persist through challenges.

A healthy mindset is crucial for financial resilience in trading. Studying historical data provides valuable insights during market downturns. Education is essential; consider enrolling in classes or courses to enhance your knowledge before venturing into the market.

It's important to acknowledge the risks involved in trading, including the potential for losses. The opinions expressed in this article are mine alone and do not represent those of a financial professional. While I found success in trading, it wasn't my primary avenue for financial growth due to the inherent risks.

Discover your passion and pursue it relentlessly. Failure is part of the journey; learn from it, persist, and strive until you succeed. Remember to seek guidance and trust in the support of the universe as you pursue your goals.

"Maintain a positive attitude. Never allow anyone to dictate what is right or wrong." It's a proven fact that successful and confident individuals consistently outperform those who are unsure of themselves and their potential for success.

Display confidence and believe in the power of positive words. Always see the glass as half full. You'll be surprised at how easily a positive attitude attracts people's attention. The two often go hand in hand. In a corporate environment, you'll notice that people prefer discussing opportunities rather than problems. They'd rather collaborate with someone who has a positive attitude, acts as a solution solver, and refrains from using the word "NO".

Learning should never cease. If you aim to succeed in your business and in life, you must listen and adapt to new ways to stay ahead of the game. Above all, maintain impeccable integrity. People want to feel secure in their ability to trust those around them. Unfortunately, in today's corporate world, some employers show little regard for their employees.

It would be wise for employers to make their employees feel valued and equal. This fosters a more functional and productive work environment. As an employer, empower your employees. You'll notice a positive response and increased productivity. This can only benefit the company and its employees at all levels.

Regardless of the industry, working together as equals in harmony can only enhance production and enable the corporation to surpass its expectations. The old saying, "Give a little and you'll get a lot in return," holds true. When employees excel at their jobs, the company prospers. Happy employees are more productive and feel empowered. They'll have a passion for listening, learning, and growing to become the best they can be. And never forget to express gratitude and give thanks each and every day.

We all understand that life is a continuous learning process. To be successful in life and in business, it's crucial to educate yourself and your coworkers to make better decisions and provide them with the freedom to make those decisions. However, it's equally important to be there to guide them in the right direction.

Teach your employees the importance of prioritizing customers. Hold power meetings and encourage your employees to contribute their ideas. Considering their ideas can significantly impact success or failure. I have been a customer of my neighborhood bank for many years. I remember when the bank employees would address you by your first name and offer suggestions on how to invest your money to see your account grow. This personal touch made customers feel valued and trusted that the bank employees had their best interests in mind.

I have observed significant changes in banking today. Machines have taken over, and the personal touch has diminished. I expressed my concerns to the bank supervisor about the potential job loss due to automation, but sadly, she was not concerned and believed it would never happen. This lack of concern is troubling, as we must all be mindful of the future and how it will impact our lives. Employers often seek ways to cut costs by replacing humans with machines, prioritizing the bottom line above all else.

The most crucial aspect is treating customers as you would like to be treated. A little special treatment can go a long way. Employers should not find it challenging to show concern and kindness to their employees. This approach empowers employees to go the extra mile in their work, creating a win-win situation for everyone.

It's not a complicated concept. When you show kindness, the universe seems to respond in your favor. It's like a chain reaction, starting with you and continuing to connect with others until it comes back to you. It's the circle of life. Do good to others, and kindness will return to you.

Share, and wealth will find its way to you. Remember always to be grateful and thankful.

It has been proven that a great and positive attitude makes all the difference in the world. In business, you need to be friendly, take a personal interest in your customers, and make them feel special. Be a problem solver and have an open mind to any ideas your customers may have. To succeed in life and achieve wealth, you need to understand when to reach out for help. Remember, we are always learning new things in life.

Interact with your staff and give them the opportunity to manage your business. Provide them with more responsibility to make decisions. Your employees will be motivated to exceed their expectations. A well-run business involves working together, trusting each other, and allowing your staff to perform at their best and make decisions that benefit the business. Empowering them to go the extra mile is a positive outcome.

Before you decide to start your own business, you need to ensure that you are the best you can be. It's a learning experience from the day you start working until the day you leave to become your own boss. Keep your feet on the ground and maintain a level head. Don't become unreachable.

Remember where you came from, no matter how wealthy you become. Recall how humble you felt when you got your first job and how grateful you were for the chance to prove yourself to your boss. Expect the same level of dedication from your staff.

The universe gives and takes. You are expected to receive and must give back. Your gratitude goes a long way. Just keep in mind that you are not alone in this universe. Be grateful each and every day, giving thanks for what you have accomplished in life, or rather, what you were allowed to accomplish in your life.

Chapter 17:
Adapting Healthy Habits

Let's discuss practicing good habits. There's been talk that for us seniors, social security will end around the year 2035. Given the corruption in our government, I'm not surprised to hear this news. Taxes are at an all-time high, yet our government struggles to do right by the working class. The younger generation isn't saving enough for retirement; they say life is short, and they want to enjoy it now. While I agree, being unprepared for the future can lead to a difficult life when you're no longer able to earn. Homelessness is rampant, and despite resources, our leaders often fail to act. They're all talk and no action, prioritizing their pockets over helping the homeless and working class.

I'm not advocating for stopping living, but we must be proactive and financially literate. Saving even just 10% won't hinder your current lifestyle. Investing in a reliable financial program allows your money to work for you. Life follows a circle: born, cared for by parents, then entering adulthood. Before you know it, you're a senior ready to retire, wondering where the years went. It's crucial to prepare for retirement while young; it's never too early to start saving. Educate yourself, make wise investments, and let your money grow over time.

In your golden years, you should live without worrying about money. But failing to prepare in youth leaves little room for correction in old age. Take the time now to make smart financial decisions. Saving for retirement doesn't require much, but it ensures a more enjoyable and fulfilling life later on. And always remember to be thankful and grateful each day.

In writing this book, it has stirred up some poignant memories. During my tenure at my family business, I often took breaks outside for some fresh air. Each day, I couldn't help but notice an elderly woman, likely in her 70s or 80s, pass by. One day, she stopped to talk to me.

She explained that her monthly social security check wasn't enough to cover her expenses. She asked if I could loan her some money, promising to repay me at the beginning of the following month when she received her next check. Though I didn't expect her to keep her promise, I was pleasantly surprised when she did, promptly paying me back on the 1st of the month.

This ritual continued for some time, and I developed a soft spot in my heart for her. She could have been someone's grandmother, and I doubted she had much family support. Her situation left her financially strapped for the last two weeks of each month, prompting me to lend her money regularly.

The significance of this sad tale serves as a reminder of the importance of achieving financial security. It became a pivotal moment in my life, motivating me to remain vigilant and financially prepared. I made a vow to myself that I wouldn't allow such a predicament to befall me, or anyone else for that matter.

There's a saying: "When you're young, investing in a sound financial program can yield significant returns as you age and are unable to work." My lesson was learned through that old lady, and I hope it serves as a lesson for you too. Stay ahead of the curve, make prudent choices, and reap the rewards in the long run.

Keep an open mind, be receptive to the lessons life presents, and make informed decisions. Gratitude should be a constant companion, and don't hesitate to lend a helping hand when you can, for it will surely come back to you manifold.

As I write my book, it strikes me that today is September 11, 2018. Seventeen years have passed since the tragic events of that day, yet the memories remain vivid in our minds. We must never forget the significance of that day. As Americans, we must stand united to ensure that such a tragedy never occurs again. Regardless of our opinions about the president, it's essential to recognize that he is prioritizing our interests. These are undoubtedly tumultuous and perilous times, but it's all the more reason for us to take control of our safety and financial well-being.

It's evident that the majority of our leaders are not adequately addressing the concerns of the middle working class taxpayers or the issue of homelessness. Instead, they seem content to obstruct progress and propagate falsehoods to undermine the positive initiatives undertaken by the president. Therefore, it's imperative for us to take charge of our lives and our families' financial futures.

While it's important to live in the present, we must also maintain a vigilant focus on our finances. We need to shield ourselves from distractions and stay committed to the path that leads to financial security. Despite the challenges faced over the past few decades, I firmly believe that better days lie ahead, particularly for the middle working class taxpayers.

Now is the time to stay resilient, maintain a positive attitude, and actively manage our finances. Seeking guidance from a financial professional can help us navigate the complexities and choose the best financial plan for ourselves and our families. By doing so, we can pave the way for a comfortable retirement and enjoy our golden years to the fullest.

Let's cultivate a spirit of gratitude and express it whenever possible, acknowledging the blessings in our lives.

Chapter 18:
Navigating Financial Challenges

We find ourselves in 2019 amidst uncertainty. Relying on the government is not a viable option. If they can't resolve their own issues, they surely can't solve ours. While senators and congresspersons enjoy lifetime security, we must take charge of our own lives and secure our destinies. Long-term thinking is crucial.

Consider a hypothetical scenario: politicians, unable to agree on laws, opt to shut down the government. We, the people who elected them, have no say. The only ones affected are government employees, working without pay temporarily. While they'll eventually receive back pay, they face immediate financial hardships.

This underscores the importance of planning ahead and pursuing financial security through education and training. You are the only person you can truly rely on. You may not control external circumstances, but you can shape your destiny and that of your family. Stay committed and grateful; you'll receive what's essential.

Experts suggest saving six months' worth of pay to weather any storm. The story of government employees going without pay for weeks illustrates this need. Education and connecting with successful individuals are vital. Learn from their experiences and struggles; success often comes after persistence and a positive attitude.

Belief in oneself and a higher power, coupled with perseverance, leads to accomplishment. Stay humble, grateful, and open to seeking help. Believe in your capabilities, and you'll receive what you desire. All that's required is faith.

We are currently in a time where our commander-in-chief has been working to assist the working class by reducing taxes, removing restrictions, and encouraging companies to return to America. The results are evident: more jobs are available than there are people, and hourly rates have risen. It's a moment to seize and commit yourself to the path of financial wealth. Educate yourself to stay on course and achieve financial stability. In the preceding chapter of this book, I outlined the amount you would need to save for retirement. However, due to the rising cost of living and longer lifespans, the formula has changed. Now, it's recommended to save 25 to 30 times your annual salary. For example, if you earn $60,000 a year, you would need to save approximately 30 times that amount, which equals $1,800,000.

The housing market is a clear indicator of the increasing cost of living, and it's expected to become even more expensive in the future. Overcome your obstacles, and success in life is within reach. Keep an open mind and never assume that the government will take care of you; that's unlikely to happen. A prime example is the current concern of the Democrats—there are no guarantees. If you remain focused on achieving your goals for your golden years, nothing can stop you.

In America, millionaires are individuals who aspire to be wealthy, acquire knowledge, and possess the necessary tools for success. Desire, knowledge, and tools are the key ingredients. The pursuit of wealth is a shared interest among the wealthiest and most famous individuals worldwide. Business owners earn millions by running their own companies. Desire is the most crucial factor in achieving wealth, but remember, the most cost-effective method of wealth creation is building a business that provides continuous income, even after retirement. It's important to recognize that millionaires are individuals who have reached the pinnacle, faced setbacks, but persevered to regain their success. The desire to become a millionaire teaches resilience and persistence, making all the difference. To be a winner, understand that you, and only you, control your life and your family's life.

It has been my experience, as demonstrated by others time and time again, that you can make millions with or without a college education, as I mentioned earlier in this book. While some people benefit from traditional brick-and-mortar universities, others thrive through real-life experiences and assignments. I am not against college education, but real-life education offers a different learning experience for some individuals. Not everyone is suited for college, and incorporating real-life education courses alongside traditional education could be beneficial. These courses focus on practical skills that are essential for success in the real world.

Learning from winners involves avoiding repeating the same mistakes repeatedly. What you make is important, but what you keep matters even more. Protecting your assets is crucial, and educating yourself on strategies to retain more of your assets, such as investing in tax-deferred programs, is essential. Consulting a financial professional can guide you in selecting the right financial program to keep more of your hard-earned money and protect your assets for retirement.

For younger generations interested in buying their first home, there are creative ways to achieve this goal. Despite college loans, there are avenues to enter the real estate market. For instance, if you work for a large corporation, you may have the opportunity to invest in a 401K, with the employer matching dollar for dollar. Maximize this opportunity over a few years, as it not only puts you in a lower tax bracket but also builds your 401K. Consult your financial expert to explore borrowing from your 401K to initiate the home-buying process. While there are associated interests, the interest paid is returned to you, making it a favorable move. Thinking outside the box can lead to smart investments that benefit your future.

In these times, maintaining a positive mindset, making smart decisions, and pursuing your goals with determination are essential. America is the land of opportunity, and with hard work and education, you can achieve your dreams. Don't hesitate to seek help and advice from others, as many minds have positive ideas that can assist you on your journey. Be grateful each day for the opportunities presented to you.

Currently, we find ourselves in the years 2017 to 2020, a period of economic prosperity where employment opportunities abound and corporations are returning to America. The younger generation has a favorable environment to pursue their aspirations. Whether working for a corporation or as an entrepreneur, it is crucial to allocate a small portion of earnings towards retirement planning. With uncertainty surrounding the future of social security, taking control of one's finances is paramount.

Investing in financial security during younger years is essential to safeguarding one's retirement. Sacrifices made now can yield significant benefits in later years when financial stability becomes crucial. Let us strive to maintain our country's prosperity and cherish the freedoms we enjoy as Americans. Respect for our nation leads to reciprocity, allowing us to pursue our goals and provide for our families. Cultivating a spirit of mutual care and gratitude fosters a positive environment where everyone thrives.

Furthermore, with our nation experiencing a period of positivity, it is opportune to invest in ourselves and our country's future. Making wise investment decisions early on ensures a comfortable lifestyle in retirement. Seek education and guidance from financial experts to navigate the complexities of financial planning. Being transparent about your aspirations, optimistic in your approach, and respectful of others' time is essential. Humility and courtesy go a long way in fostering positive relationships and receiving assistance when needed.

Expressing gratitude for the opportunities and accomplishments in life empowers individuals to continue striving for success. Let us embrace a mindset of gratitude as we navigate our financial journeys and express appreciation for the blessings bestowed upon us.

To the younger generation, I urge you to be wise and avoid enslaving your life to addiction, debt, and premature parenthood without the means to support a family. Make time for self-care and don't hesitate to seek help when needed. When entering the workforce, make sound decisions to make your job easier and take advantage of the benefits offered by your employer. Focus on long-term planning, adjusting expenses to fit your lifestyle, and consider provisions for personal savings, investments, and additional sources of income.

For seniors nearing retirement, I've estimated my social security, pension, and annuity, along with income from reliable rental properties. You can estimate your benefits by contacting social security for monthly projections. Creating a life worksheet has helped me stay in control of my finances, ensuring I live within my means and use common sense. Seek assistance from professional financial advisors to make informed decisions.

In America, you have the freedom to achieve anything. Dream big and aim high; there's nothing you can't accomplish with determination and focus. The secret is to find a formula to ensure you never run out of cash. As we're living longer, concerns about financial security in retirement are common among older Americans. Fortunately, many baby boomers have consulted financial planners to mitigate these risks. However, the current generation often relies on the government for financial support, despite evidence to the contrary. It's crucial for them to realize the importance of self-education and proactive financial planning for a secure future.

While life may seem great when you're young, financial challenges become more daunting as you age. Remember, there's no one else to rely on but yourself. Our government may not prioritize the welfare of taxpayers, so it's essential to take control of your financial future. Stay vigilant and proactive in securing your financial well-being.

Making Your Money Last a Lifetime

GUARANTEED INCOME		
Social Security	$ _____	
Pension/annuity	$ _____	
Net rental income		$ _____
Salary (weekly/biweekly)	$ _____	
Other		$ _____
TOTAL ANNUAL GUARANTEED INCOME	$ _____	

ADD UP SAVINGS & INVESTMENTS		
Saving/ Checking Accounts	$ _____	
Certificates of Deposit	$ _____	
IRAs	$ _____	
401(k)s & 403(b)s		$ _____
Other investment accounts	$ _____	
SUBTOTAL: SPENDABLE ASSETS	$ _____	
Subtract cash (one or two years worth of expenses not covered by guaranteed income)		$ _____
GET YOUR NET SPENDABLE ASSETS		$ _____

TOTAL UP INITIAL ANNUAL INCOME		
Add guaranteed income (step 1) to income from assets (step 2)	$ _____	

DETERMINE YOUR INITIAL MONTHLY INCOME		
Divide total annual income (step 3) by 12		$ _____

And you are done!

Cash Flow Sheet

INCOME	Planned	Actual
Salary 1 (after truces)	$ _____	$ _____
Salary 2 (after truces)	$ _____	$ _____
Other income	$ _____	$ _____
Other income	$ _____	$ _____
Total Income	$ _____	$ _____

EXPENDITURES		
Nest egg	$ _____	$ _____
(min. 10% of total incl. JTTJe)		
Charitable Donations	$ _____	$ _____
Mortgage or Rent	$ _____	$ _____
Food	$ _____	$ _____
Utilities	$ _____	$ _____
Auto Payments	$ _____	$ _____
Misc. Auto Expense	$ _____	$ _____
Repair	$ _____	$ _____
Maintenance	$ _____	$ _____
Gas	$ _____	$ _____
Auto Insurance	$ _____	$ _____
Life Insurance	$ _____	$ _____
Home Owner's Insurance	$ _____	$ _____
Medical Insurance	$ _____	$ _____
Clothing	$ _____	$ _____
Debt Payments	$ _____	$ _____
Misc. Expenses	$ _____	$ _____
TOTAL EXPENDITURES	$ _____	$ _____
Income Less Expenditures	$ _____	$ _____

Cash Flow For *Date:*_______

Net Flow Sheet

ASSETS Current Liquid Assets	
Cash (on hand)	$____
Checking Account	$____
Savings Account	$____
Certificates	$____
Money Owed You	$____
Tax Refund Due	$____
Life Insurance (Cash Value)	$____
Stocks/Bonds	$____
Mutual Fund Shares	$____
Precious Metals	$____
Other ________	$____
Other ________	$____
Total Current Assets	$____
FIXED ASSETS	
Home	$____
Automobiles	$____
Furniture	$____
Jewelry	$____
Personal Property	$____
Other ________	$____
Total Fixed Assets	$____
DEFERRED ASSETS	
Retirement Plan	$____
I.R.A.	$____
Other ________	$____
Other ________	$____
Total Deferred Assets	$____
TOTAL ASSETS	$____

OTHER LIABILITIES Current Liabilities	
Charge Accounts	$____
Credit Cards	$____
Insurance Due	$____
Taxes Due	$____
Current Bills Due	$____
Line of Credit	$____
Other ________	$____
Other ________	$____
Other ________	$____
Other ________	$____
Total Current Liabilities	$____
LONG-TERM LIABILITIES	
Auto Loan # 1	$____
Auto Loan # 2	$____
Installment Loan	$____
Personal Loan	$____
Mortgage Loan	$____
Other ________	$____
Total Long-Term Liabilities	$____
TOTAL LIABILITIES	$____

As of *Date:* ________

Total Assets

$____

Total Liabilities

We have experienced three astonishing and prosperous years (2017, 2018, 2019). Unexpectedly, in 2020, COVID-19 hit our country hard, impacting the entire world. Our nation had to shut down, leading companies to furlough their employees and everyone to quarantine indoors. The world we once knew has changed, and not for the better. This underscores the importance of taking control of our own lives and making provisions to weather both good and bad times.

I have taken every possible measure to protect myself from such disasters. While it hasn't been easy, a little sacrifice before the COVID-19 outbreak made a significant difference in my ability to adjust and move forward. I found myself able to survive the economic ups and downs, having saved enough money to sustain myself and my family. This is why I've written this book—to assist anyone willing to help themselves, to take charge of their lives, and control their destiny.

It's important to note that I had no forewarning of this disaster. I was just as surprised as you and the rest of the world. We've witnessed firsthand how the leaders of our country bicker among themselves, often disregarding the suffering of taxpayers unable to pay rent or provide for their families.

However, there is a light at the end of the tunnel. We must remain strong and take care of ourselves and our families as we endure these difficult times. Regardless of whether one believes in God or not, it's comforting to know that there is hope and support available. A simple prayer, in one's own words, can carry great meaning.

Chapter 19: Conclusion

Taking Financial Responsibility: Take responsibility for your money by understanding its movements and evaluating your investments monthly. This is crucial for ensuring financial success.

Seeking Professional Advice: Invest time in consulting with financial advisers to learn where to best allocate your funds. Maintaining financial security requires vigilance and focus on your financial goals, so keep track of your finances and prioritize what matters most to you and your family.

Promoting Financial Literacy: To control spending, limit the number of credit cards you use. Additionally, involve your children in positive financial decision-making and encourage them to save money responsibly. This starts at home and applies even after retirement. Simplify your investments for easier management and seek professional advice for optimal results.

Strength Through Adversity: Stay strong during difficult times and make informed decisions while taking responsibility for your actions. Always maintain belief in yourself and trust in a higher power, remembering to appreciate the blessings in your life.

Long-Term Wealth Building: Embrace a disciplined approach to savings and investments. Start by saving a small portion of each paycheck, which will help you grow your wealth over time. Commit to long-term financial strategies that will provide stability and support you through life's challenges and successes.

Many people seek quick ways to become wealthy, but my mother's advice proved invaluable: saving a portion of every paycheck fosters the patience needed to grow wealth over time. From my first job, I diligently set aside a small percentage of my earnings, establishing a lifelong habit of saving through both prosperous and challenging times.

I adopted a long-term investment strategy, allocating funds to stocks, mutual funds, and everyday savings accounts. Witnessing the gradual growth of these investments over time was rewarding. They not only supported me during retirement but also provided the means to make improvements to my home.

Navigating through both tough and prosperous periods, I learned invaluable lessons. Chief among them was the importance of living within my means and the challenges that come with it. Additionally, I realized the significance of expanding my financial avenues rather than merely maintaining them.

My experience underscores a simple truth: by consistently setting aside a portion of your paycheck, you, too, can cultivate your wealth over time.

We all strive to improve our physical health and well-being, but it's equally important to boost our financial fitness. Understanding your credit score is essential for assessing your financial health, as it reflects your history of repaying loans and debts. This three-digit number, assigned by credit agencies, is influenced by various factors such as the length of your credit history.

Here's how credit scores typically evolve with age:

- In your 20s, your score may range from 600 to 662, as it takes time to establish a credit history. Consistently paying bills on time will help raise your score.
- By your 30s, you should aim for a score in the high six hundreds (675).
- In your 40s, target a score in the higher six hundreds (685 or higher).
- In your 50s, strive for a score in the seven hundreds (710).
- By your 60s, aim for a high seven hundred score

(750).

While these scores are considered average, aiming for excellence is crucial. Make timely payments, monitor your credit score regularly, and keep credit card balances low. It's important to keep all accounts open, even if not frequently used, to maintain a healthy credit history. Avoid opening too many accounts, as this can negatively impact your credit score.

In conclusion, remember that life is about more than just financial wealth. It's about faith, love, and relationships with family and others. Giving back, practicing gratitude, and finding balance are essential principles to live by. Those who constantly seek more without appreciating what they have will never find true contentment or wealth.

Always remember:

- Keep God in your life.
- Be grateful.
- Give back.
- Love one another.
- Maintain balance in your life.
- Understand that karma influences every aspect of your life, including your financial well-being.

Made in the USA
Columbia, SC
16 September 2026

d73cb1dc-384d-4047-8ee5-912f20dfeda0R01